P9-CMS-637

CHARLIE BROWN'S 'CYCLOPEDIA

Super Questions and Answers and Amazing Facts

Featuring Planes and Other Things that Fly

Volume 6

Based on the Charles M. Schulz Characters

Funk & Wagnalls, Inc.

Photograph and Illustration Credits: American Airlines, 264, 282, 283; American Hall of Aviation History, Northrup University, 246, 247, 261; Marc Bulka/Sipa Press/Black Star, ix; British Airways, 273; Cessna Aircraft Company, 269, 270; Peter Dickerson/Editorial Photocolor Archives, 251; Editorial Photocolor Archives, 254; Eleanor Ehrhardt, 268, 280; Kennebec Valley Chamber of Commerce/Paul Fournier, 279; McDonnell Douglas Corporation, 278; National Aeronautics and Space Administration, 285, 286; New York City Fire Department Photo Unit, 277; New York State Department of Commerce, 245, 250; Sikorsky Aircraft Division of United Technologies, 276; Smithsonian Institution, National Air and Space Museum, 242, 253, 257, 258; Mike Sheil/Black Star, xi; U.S. Air Force, 252, 257, 260, 274, 275.

Copyright © 1980 by United Feature Syndicate, Inc. Produced in association with Charles M. Schulz Creative Associates. All rights reserved under International and Pan-American Copyright Conventions. Published in the United States by Random House, Inc., New York, and simultaneously in Canada by Random House of Canada Limited, Toronto. Distributed by Funk & Wagnalls, Inc., New York, N.Y. Manufactured in the United States of America.
ISBN: 0–394–84555–2   3 4 5 6 7 8 9 0

A large part of the material in this volume was previously published in *Charlie Brown's Second Super Book of Questions and Answers.*

Introduction

Welcome to volume 6 of *Charlie Brown's 'Cyclopedia*! Have you ever wondered how people first tried to fly, or what a blimp is, or how a heavy airplane can stay up in the air? Charlie Brown and the rest of the *Peanuts* gang are here to help you find the answers to these questions and many more about planes and other things that fly. Have fun!

Charlie Brown in the Air

RIGHT ON!

WING POWER

How did people first try to fly?

People made wings of feathers and tried to fly like birds. They attached their homemade wings to their arms and jumped from high places. Usually they were killed or badly injured.

In 1490, an Italian named Danti made some wings. For a moment it looked as if they would work. But Danti crashed to the ground. He was seriously hurt.

John Damian lived in Scotland. He made wings of feathers, too. In 1507, he jumped from the top of a castle. He fell and broke his leg.

Wan Ho lived in China in about 1500. He was very brave. He tried to rocket through space. He tied 47 rockets to the back of his chair. Then he strapped himself in. Some friends attached two kites to his chair. They lit the rockets. There was a great big explosion and lots of smoke. Wan Ho was never seen again.

Who is Icarus?

Icarus is the unfortunate hero of an ancient Greek story. His father made wings of feathers for him. The feathers were glued together with wax. "Be careful," warned his father. "Don't fly too near the sun or the wax will melt." But according to the legend, Icarus didn't listen to his father. Instead, he flew near the warm rays of the sun and the wax melted. Feathers fell from Icarus' wings, and he plunged into the sea and drowned.

What was the first successful flying machine?

The first successful flying machine was a balloon built by Joseph and Jacques Montgolfier (ZHOCK mawn-gawl-FYAY) in 1782. The brothers were watching a fire burning in their fireplace. They noticed that the smoke went up the chimney. They watched other fires and saw that smoke always went up. The brothers wondered why. They decided that there must be something special about smoke. Joseph and Jacques trapped some smoke in a paper bag. It was a risky thing to do. The bag could have caught fire. But it didn't. It floated in the air.

On June 5, they took a bag that measured 35 feet (11 meters) around. It weighed 300 pounds (135 kilograms). The brothers made a smoky fire by burning straw. They floated the bag over the fire. It rose more than a mile (almost 2 kilometers) high before it cooled off and came back down. This was the first balloon flight.

Later, people discovered that it was heat and not smoke that made balloons rise.

The first Montgolfier balloon

How does the hot-air balloon work?

A hot-air balloon is a large, airtight cloth or plastic bag filled with heated air. Hot air is lighter than cool air. So hot air rises. The hot air inside the balloon is lighter than the cool air outside, so the balloon rises. When the heated air cools and becomes as heavy as the air outside, the balloon will stop rising and come down.

A balloon carries heavy weights in a basket that is tied to its bottom end. The weights are usually bags of sand. When the weights are thrown out, the balloon starts to rise. As more and more weights are thrown out, the balloon rises higher. When the passengers want to come down, they can open the top of the bag to let out heated air.

Hot-air balloons are open at the bottom. They are filled with hot air by lighting a gas burner underneath the opening. Today most balloons are not filled with hot air. Gases that are lighter than air are used instead. Helium is a lighter-than-air gas that is often used.

Early balloons carried sponges and a bucket of water for putting out the fires that kept starting!

THAT'S MY SISTER LUCY. SHE LOVES TO MAKE A GRAND ENTRANCE!

243

Who was the first person to fly?

Pilâtre de Rozier (pee-LAH-truh duh raw-ZYAY) of France was the first person to fly. A duck, a sheep, and a rooster had already flown in a Montgolfier balloon. Now it was man's turn. King Louis XVI (the sixteenth) offered to send up a prisoner who was supposed to die soon. But de Rozier begged to go instead.

On October 15, 1783, Pilâtre de Rozier climbed aboard the balloon. It rose 80 feet (24 meters) into the air, about as high as a six-story building. It probably would have gone higher, but it was held down by a rope. Man's first flight lasted 4½ minutes. The balloon weighed 1,600 pounds (more than 700 kilograms).

How fast can a balloon go?

A balloon has no moving power of its own. It can travel only as fast as the wind that carries it.

Why did people stop using balloons for travel?

Balloon flight can't be controlled. Some people tried to steer balloons by using sails. Others tried oars. A few people tried paddles. Nothing worked. When better airships were invented, people lost interest in balloons.

How are balloons used today?

Scientists use very big plastic balloons to gather weather information. Balloons carry equipment to record temperature, humidity (moisture), air pressure, and wind speeds. This information is sent back to the scientists by radio equipment carried by the balloons.

If a weather balloon breaks, the instruments it carries float back to earth in a bright red parachute.

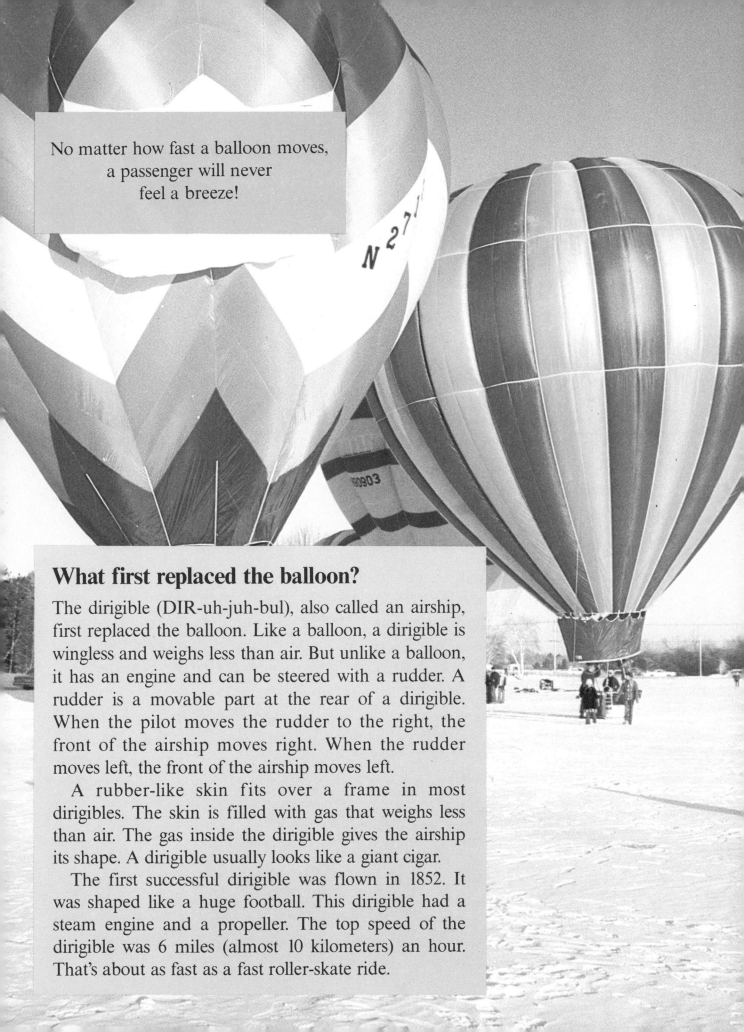

No matter how fast a balloon moves,
a passenger will never
feel a breeze!

What first replaced the balloon?

The dirigible (DIR-uh-juh-bul), also called an airship, first replaced the balloon. Like a balloon, a dirigible is wingless and weighs less than air. But unlike a balloon, it has an engine and can be steered with a rudder. A rudder is a movable part at the rear of a dirigible. When the pilot moves the rudder to the right, the front of the airship moves right. When the rudder moves left, the front of the airship moves left.

A rubber-like skin fits over a frame in most dirigibles. The skin is filled with gas that weighs less than air. The gas inside the dirigible gives the airship its shape. A dirigible usually looks like a giant cigar.

The first successful dirigible was flown in 1852. It was shaped like a huge football. This dirigible had a steam engine and a propeller. The top speed of the dirigible was 6 miles (almost 10 kilometers) an hour. That's about as fast as a fast roller-skate ride.

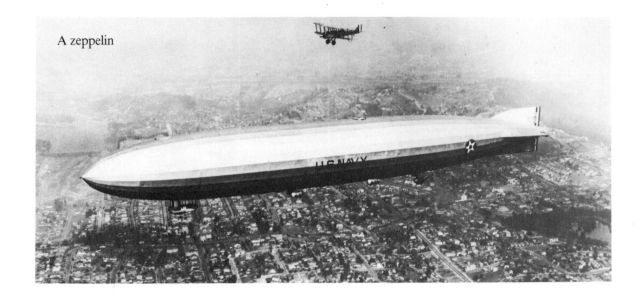

A zeppelin

What was a zeppelin?

A zeppelin was a large dirigible. It was named for the man who designed it, Count Ferdinand von Zeppelin of Germany.

The first zeppelin was built in 1900. It had a cigar-shaped aluminum frame. It weighed 25,350 pounds (11,408 kilograms), about as much as two large male elephants.

How were zeppelins used?

Zeppelins carried passengers who wanted to go sightseeing. Regularly scheduled zeppelin trips flew across the Atlantic Ocean. Count von Zeppelin began an airline company that carried 34,288 people in four years without an accident. During World War I zeppelins had another use. One hundred zeppelins were built for war. Their mission—bombing London!

In 1928 the Graf Zeppelin flew around the world in 22 days!

"AROUND THE WORLD IN 22 DAYS"...I WONDER IF I COULD WRITE A SONG ABOUT THAT??!

What was the Hindenburg?

The Hindenburg was the largest airship ever built. It was a zeppelin 803 feet (241 meters) long. That's about as long as 54 taxis in a line. The Hindenburg was 135 feet (more than 40 meters) wide. That's about as long as 9 taxis in a line. The Hindenburg had a lounge, a piano, and paneled bedrooms. It made 35 trips across the Atlantic Ocean. On May 6, 1937, it suddenly exploded and burned as it was trying to land at Lakehurst, New Jersey. There were 97 people aboard. Thirty-six of them died. No one ever found out what caused the disaster. But zeppelins were filled with hydrogen gas, which people knew was very explosive. After the Hindenburg tragedy, hydrogen was never used in airships again. And zeppelins were never again manufactured.

The Hindenburg

Will zeppelins ever be used again?

Perhaps zeppelins will be used again in the future. Scientists today are beginning to think about lighter-than-air aircraft once again. A zeppelin, powered by the most powerful energy in the world—atomic energy—might work well. Atomic energy uses very little fuel. An atomic zeppelin would not have to be refueled very often. It could remain in the air for a week at a time. Zeppelins can stay still in the sky. A zeppelin could remain in one place while scientists studied the land and water below. Some people are sure that zeppelins will make a comeback.

What is a blimp used for?

There are only four blimps in existence today. They are owned by the Goodyear Rubber Company. They are used for advertising. You can't help noticing a Goodyear Blimp when it cruises in the sky.

Blimps are small dirigibles. They are usually filled with helium gas. Blimp is a nickname. The first model was called an A-Limp. The B-Limp was an improved ship. Later its name was shortened to blimp.

When was the parachute invented?

No one knows exactly when the parachute was invented. The idea for what we now call a parachute is a very old one.

Chin Shih Huang Ti (cheen shur hoo-WANG DEE) ruled China about 2,100 years ago. He liked to jump from the Great Wall of China carrying an open umbrella over his head. The umbrella slowed the emperor's fall. He was never hurt.

Sébastien Lenormand (say-bah-STYAN luh-nor-MAWN) built a 14-foot (4-meter) chute. He used it in 1783, to jump from a tower. He claimed he had just invented a way of escaping from burning apartment houses. A few years later, daring balloonists began doing stunts with parachutes. Sometimes they carried parachutes just for protection in case their balloons burst into flames.

248

How does a parachute work?

An open parachute looks like a big umbrella. As a parachute falls to earth, the air underneath pushes upward against it. This push slows its fall. The umbrella part is attached to long lines. The lines are attached to straps around the jumper's body. The parachute is folded up in a small pack. It is strapped to the jumper's back. When the jumper leaps into the air, usually from an airplane, he or she pulls a string called the ripcord. That makes the parachute open. Sometimes the ripcord is hooked to a line inside the plane. In this case, when the jumper jumps out, the ripcord is pulled automatically. The rushing air fills the chute out into its umbrella shape and slows it down. Even so, the jumper hits the ground at about 15 miles (24 kilometers) an hour. It's a lot like jumping from a moving car.

Sometimes parachutes are attached to the tails of big, fast airplanes. The parachutes pop out behind the airplanes. This helps to slow the planes down when they are landing. Parachutes also pop out and help to slow down spacecraft returning to earth.

What is skydiving?

Skydiving is a popular modern sport. Skydivers carry parachutes and jump from planes that are often as high as 12,500 feet (3,750 meters) in the air. Skydivers do stunts in the sky for about a minute before they open their parachutes. They do loops, turns, barrel rolls, and more. Sometimes a group of skydivers will join hands and form a circle.

Skydivers open their parachutes when they are no less than 2,500 feet (750 meters) above the ground. They float to earth at 12 miles (about 19 kilometers) an hour. Skydiving is the fastest-growing sport in America.

 Before skydivers open their parachutes, they can float through the air at 200 miles (320 kilometers) an hour! That's nearly four times as fast as a car on a highway!

How does a glider plane fly?

A glider is an airplane without an engine. It is usually towed up into the air by an engine-powered airplane. The two are connected by a tow rope. When the rope is released, the glider flies through currents of rising air. The air pushes the glider up. The currents may be warm air rising from hot, flat areas of the earth. Or they may be wind currents that have been turned upward after hitting a hillside.

Without the air currents, called "updrafts," the motorless glider would settle down to earth. Even the biggest engine-powered airplanes act like gliders when they come in for a landing.

What is hang gliding?

Hang gliding is a popular American sport. The person gliding wears a harness which is attached to a glider. The glider looks something like a huge kite. It is shaped like a triangle. At its widest point, a glider is about as wide as a car is long. The pilot holds on to the glider and races down a hill into the wind. Or else the pilot jumps off a cliff. The wind lifts the glider into the air. The pilot uses a control bar to change directions. A hang glider usually travels as fast as a car would travel on a busy street. A person learning to hang glide usually flies 10–20 feet (3–6 meters) above the earth. That's about as high as a one-story building. After a while an experienced pilot may take the glider up higher. Hang gliders never fly as high as airplanes.

Orville Wright

Wilbur Wright

Who invented the airplane?

The Wright Brothers invented the first safe, successful airplane. But their first flight, on December 17, 1903, was not great news. Nothing appeared in the newspapers on that day. A few days later, short items began to appear in newspapers across the country, but no one seemed very interested or impressed.

How long did the first airplane flight last?

Orville Wright took the "Flyer I" up in the air and flew it for 12 seconds. Wilbur Wright took turns with his brother flying their airplane. The next two flights lasted twice as long as the first one. On the fourth flight that day, the airplane stayed in the air for 59 seconds. After it landed, a sudden gust of wind tipped the plane over. "Flyer I" was badly damaged. The first successful airplane was never flown again.

Wright Brothers' takeoff

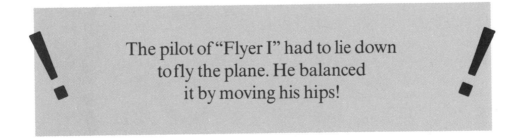

The pilot of "Flyer I" had to lie down
to fly the plane. He balanced
it by moving his hips!

Who was the first person to fly across the sea?

Louis Blériot (loo-EE blay-RYO) flew across the English Channel in 1909. He flew from France to England in a Blériot XI (eleven) monoplane. A monoplane has only one set of wings. Most early planes had two sets—one above the other.

Blériot's flight was historic. He proved that people from different countries could now visit each other fairly easily.

Blériot monoplane

Who was the first woman pilot?

Baroness de la Roche (duh lah RAWSH) was the first woman pilot. She made her first flight in 1908. Two years later, Baroness de la Roche received a pilot's license.

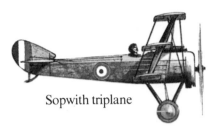
Sopwith triplane

Nieuport 28

Nieuport 17

How were planes first used to help fight a war?

Airplanes were first used for war in October 1911. During the Italo-Turkish War, an Italian pilot flew over enemy lands. He wanted to see what the enemy was doing. The first bombing raid came a few days later. An Italian pilot dropped four grenades over Turkish lands. He also scattered leaflets in the air. The leaflets urged the people to surrender.

Albatros D.3   Fokker D.8

What are dogfights?

Dogfights are airplane sky battles. They were common during World War I, which began in 1914. Squadrons of 10 to 20 planes fought each other in the sky. The planes twisted and turned in many directions as each pilot tried to shoot the enemy. A pilot would try to get behind an enemy plane before firing his guns. This kept him safe from bullets, but close enough to hit the enemy.

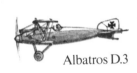

What was barnstorming?

Barnstorming was a type of show that stunt pilots gave in the early days of airplanes. Barnstorming pilots flew their planes from small town to small town, stopping wherever a fair or festival was going on. A pilot caught people's attention by performing daring acrobatic stunts and swooping low over the town and nearby farms. Airplanes were an unusual sight. So crowds soon gathered to watch the pilot's daring feats. Then the pilot landed his plane in a field and sold tickets for rides in the plane. Usually a quick air tour around the town cost five dollars.

The famous pilot Charles Lindbergh got his start in 1922 by helping barnstorming pilots attract crowds. Lindbergh performed parachute jumps and walked on the wings of flying planes!

256

What made Charles Lindbergh famous?

Charles Lindbergh was the first person to fly alone across the Atlantic Ocean. Raymond Orteig, a New York City hotel owner, offered $25,000 to the first person to fly nonstop from New York to Paris. Charles Lindbergh wanted to be that person.

On May 20, 1927, Lindbergh took off early in the morning from Garden City, New York. He flew his plane, the "Spirit of St. Louis," through fog, rain, and sleet. He landed in Paris 33 hours and 30 minutes later. He had flown 3,600 miles (nearly 5,800 kilometers).

"Spirit of St. Louis"

National Air and Space Museum

Where can you see the "Spirit of St. Louis"?

You can see Lindbergh's airplane at the National Air and Space Museum in Washington, D.C. After Lindbergh made his famous flight to Paris, he sent the "Spirit" back to the United States on a Navy ship. He flew it on a victory tour of Latin America. Then he flew the "Spirit" to Washington and gave it to the Smithsonian Institution. At the National Air and Space Museum, which is a branch of the Smithsonian, you can see not only the "Spirit of St. Louis," but also the Wright brothers' "Flyer" and many other famous airplanes and spacecraft.

What is a "flying ace"?

A flying ace is a pilot who has shot down five or more enemy planes.

Who was the Red Baron?

The Red Baron was Baron von Richthofen (RIKHT-hoe-fun) of Germany. He shot down 80 planes during World War I. That made him the greatest flying ace of all time. He was called the Red Baron because his plane was colored red. Sometimes he was known as the Red Knight. His flying squadron was known as Richthofen's Flying Circus.

Who was Amelia Earhart?

Amelia Earhart was a famous pilot. She was the first woman to travel as an airplane passenger across the Atlantic Ocean. She was also the first woman—and the second pilot—to fly across the Atlantic alone. To prepare for this long solo flight, she practiced going without sleep or food for many days at a time. Her flight from Newfoundland to Ireland took only about 14 hours. Amelia Earhart won many awards for her flying, including the Distinguished Flying Cross.

What finally happened to Amelia Earhart?

In 1937, she and Fred Noonan tried to fly a twin-engine airplane around the world. A ship picked up a radio signal from their airplane. They were short of fuel over the Pacific Ocean. Carrier planes and ships searched for them. No trace of Amelia Earhart, Fred Noonan, or their plane was ever found.

When did people start using airplanes to deliver the mail?

Some early airplane pilots and balloonists carried mail as a stunt. But the first official United States air-mail delivery was made in 1911, by Paul Beck and Earle Ovington. They delivered mail from Garden City, New York, to Jamaica, New York. This was a distance of less than 8 miles (almost 13 kilometers).

May 15, 1917, was the beginning of the first continuous air-mail service in the world. Army pilots flew military mail from different cities in Europe to New York City, Philadelphia, and Washington, D.C. Regular air-mail service from the United States to Europe began in 1918.

Today almost all mail that travels more than 100 miles (160 kilometers) goes by air.

On an average day, Kennedy International Airport in New York handles ten million five hundred thousand (10,500,000) air-mail letters!

HOW NICE... AN AIR MAIL LETTER!

What do bush pilots do?

Bush pilots fly to areas where very few people live. These areas are usually on mountains or in jungles or near the North and South poles. Bush pilots deliver food, medicine, and supplies. They take sick people to hospitals. Flying conditions are often dangerous. Winds near the poles may gust up to 100 miles (160 kilometers) an hour. Isolated areas usually don't have weather stations. So weather information is often not available. Neither are airports or landing fields, much of the time. Bush pilots sometimes have to land on ice. If the ice is too thin, the bush pilot is in trouble.

Bush pilots performed heroic deeds in the early days of flying. But today fewer regions are isolated. So the need for bush pilots is fast disappearing.

How can someone become an airplane pilot?

Every pilot has to have a license in order to fly an airplane. A person must be at least 16 years old to get a student's license, and 17 years old to get a regular license. Flying lessons are necessary, and they are expensive, too. They cost at least $600 a course. In the United States, the Federal Aviation Administration issues pilots' licenses. But first a student must pass a written test, a flying test, and an examination by a doctor.

There are many things to learn about flying. Students usually take courses in weather, air science, and the rules of flying.

A student pilot must spend at least 40 hours flying. A student learns to fly by watching an experienced pilot. He or she also learns by reading air charts and by studying the instruments on the plane. The student must complete one 100-mile (160-kilometer) flight without having the instructor in the plane.

What was the smallest airplane ever built?

The smallest airplane was the Stits Skybaby. It was built by Ray Stits in 1952. The Skybaby was about half as long as an average car.

What was the biggest airplane ever built?

The biggest airplane ever built was the H.2 "Hercules" flying boat. It measured 320 feet (96 meters) from wing tip to wing tip. It was 219 feet (66 meters) long, which is about 20 times as big as the Stits Skybaby. It cost 40 million dollars ($40,000,000) to build. It had eight engines and weighed 190 tons (171 metric tons). On a test run in Long Beach Harbor in California, it rose 10 feet (3 meters) into the air and flew 1,000 yards (900 meters). It was never flown again.

747 Luxury Liner

What was the heaviest airplane ever flown?

The heaviest airplane ever flown is a 747 that weighs more than 410 tons (about 370 metric tons). That's about as heavy as 82 elephants. Without fuel and equipment it weighs only 160 tons (144 metric tons), about the weight of 32 elephants.

How can a heavy plane stay up in the air?

When a plane is flying, it is being pulled up and down and backward and forward all at the same time. The force of "gravity" pulls the plane downward. "Lift" pushes it upward. Lift is the force made by the wings as they cut through the air. The force of "drag" pulls the plane backward, while "thrust" pushes it forward. Jet engines or propellers give thrust. A heavy plane in steady flight stays in the air for two reasons. The thrust from its engines or propellers equals the drag force. And the lift made by its wings equals the force of gravity on the plane (its weight).

LIFT

THRUST

DRAG

GRAVITY

WOW!

What are the most important parts of an airplane?

An airplane has three main parts. They are the wings, the tail assembly, and the body. The body is called the fuselage (FYOO-suh-lij).

The wings lift the airplane into the sky. Ailerons (AY-luh-ronz) are the flaps on the wings that keep the plane in a curved path during turns. Other flaps on the wings give the plane stronger lift at the slower speeds of takeoff and landing.

The tail assembly keeps the plane steady. The rudder is part of the tail assembly. The pilot can swing the rudder to the right or to the left. When it swings to the right, the front of the plane moves to the right. When it swings to the left, the front of the plane moves to the left.

The fin is another part of the tail assembly. The fin keeps the plane steady in forward flight.

The stabilizer is also part of the tail assembly. The stabilizer keeps the airplane from wobbling up and down in the air. Tail parts, called elevators, that are connected to the stabilizer help the plane go up and down when the plane takes off and lands.

The body is where the passengers and freight are carried.

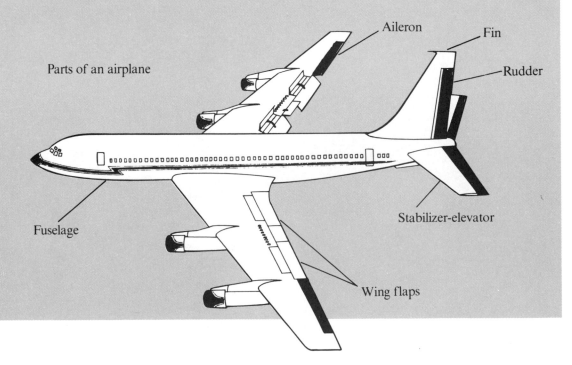

Parts of an airplane

Aileron

Fin

Rudder

Fuselage

Stabilizer-elevator

Wing flaps

How can a plane fly upside down?

A plane can fly upside down because the same forces—lift, drag, thrust, and gravity—that pull on a right-side-up plane also pull on an upside-down plane. The only force that may not be strong in an upside-down plane is lift—the force made by the wings as they cut through the air. As long as the wings have enough lift in the upside-down position, the plane will stay in the air.

But first, the ailerons—movable flaps near the tips of the wings—must turn the plane over. By moving the ailerons with a wheel or a control stick, the pilot can roll the plane over until it is moving along upside down.

What is an automatic pilot?

An automatic pilot is a set of instruments that flies the plane without any help from the human pilot. Perhaps the person flying the plane is busy. Or maybe the weather is bad. The pilot is not able to see clearly because of heavy rain, snow, or fog. Then the pilot may decide to use electronic equipment to fly the plane. The automatic pilot can keep the plane flying in a certain direction. It can keep the plane flying at a particular height in the sky. The automatic pilot can fly the plane more perfectly than a person can.

Someday flight may become completely automatic. Perhaps computers, not people, will guide airplanes through an entire flight.

What is a prop plane?

The "prop" in "prop plane" is short for propeller. A prop plane has blades in the front that spin around. These blades make up the propeller. The propeller helps to move the airplane forward.

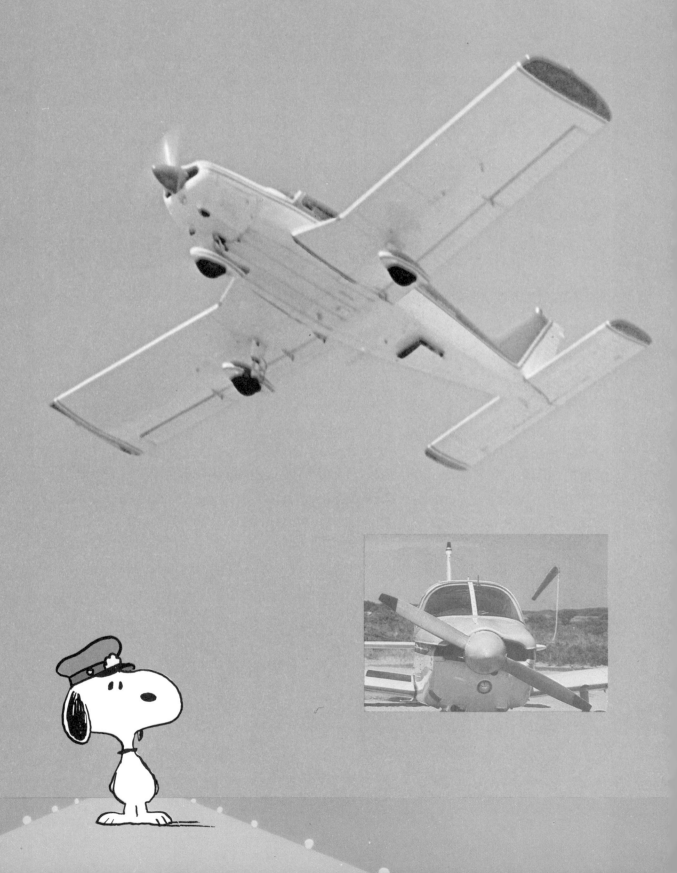

How fast can a prop plane fly?

The speed of a prop plane depends upon the size of the plane and how many engines it has. A single-engine, six-passenger plane may reach a speed of 180 miles (288 kilometers) per hour. The fastest prop plane ever built was an experimental Navy model. It was never manufactured for use. This plane reached a top speed of 670 miles (1,072 kilometers) an hour.

Crop spraying plane

What is a jet plane?

A jet plane is an aircraft that has jet engines. When fuel is burned in a jet engine, it gives off hot gases. The gases shoot out of the back of the engine in a stream, called a jet. The stream rushing out toward the rear makes the plane move forward. This forward force is called "thrust." A toy balloon filled with air shows how this works. If you suddenly let go of the stem of the balloon, the balloon will zip away. Air rushes from the stem in one direction, pushing the balloon in the other direction—just like the jet plane.

How fast can a jet plane go?

One jet reached a speed of more than 2,193 miles (3,509 kilometers) an hour. But most jets can't go that fast. A plane with two jet engines can go about 560 miles (896 kilometers) an hour. Some jets with four engines can fly faster than 1,000 miles (1,600 kilometers) an hour.

What is a "sonic boom"?

A sonic boom is the noise made by a supersonic airplane. Supersonic means faster than the speed of sound traveling through air—about 1,100 feet (330 meters) a second. When a plane is flying, waves of air build up in front of it. When a plane flies faster than the speed of sound, the waves become cone-shaped. The plane is inside the pointed tip of the cone. A cone-shaped air wave is called a shock wave. When the cone sweeps over the ground, the shock wave makes a loud noise or boom. This is called sonic boom. It can break windows and crack walls. And, over a period of time, such loud noise can damage your ears.

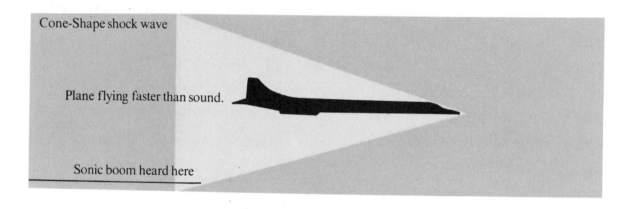

Cone-Shape shock wave

Plane flying faster than sound.

Sonic boom heard here

A "SONIC BOOM???" MY SISTER CAN CAUSE A "SONIC BOOM" WITHOUT EVER LEAVING THE LIVING ROOM...

What is the SST?

SST stands for supersonic transport. SSTs fly faster than the speed of sound. Most planes don't fly nearly that fast. The Russian Tu-144 and the French and British Concordes are supersonic planes. The Concorde flies at about 1,019 miles (about 1,630 kilometers) an hour. A Boeing 747, which is not supersonic, flies at about 595 miles (952 kilometers) an hour.

The SST is shaped like a dart. The wings are thin and swept back. When planes fly at supersonic speeds, air pressure against the fast-moving plane becomes very strong. The SST's nose comes to a sharp point so that the plane can cut through the hard pressure of the air.

A Concorde

What are the newer planes like?

Some of the newer planes are shaped differently from older airplanes. The tail assembly of a plane is usually behind the wings. But a new plane called the Avro Vulcan has a tail assembly that lines up with the wings. It does not extend behind them. The Avro Vulcan is shaped like a triangle. Each wing forms one point of the triangle. The plane's nose forms the third point.

A plane called the Northrop YB-49 has no tail assembly at all. It doesn't have a body either. The passengers, the pilot, and the crew sit inside the wings. The windows are at the edge of the wings so people can look out. The plane is very thick in the middle. The tips of the wings are swept back. The large wings do the work of the tail assembly. They keep the plane steady.

The HL-10 is a wingless plane. It flies by rocket power. It travels at a speed of 610 miles (976 kilometers) an hour as it climbs in the air. When it reaches flying height, the HL-10 moves forward at 1,200 miles (1,920 kilometers) an hour.

The "YB-49," jet-propelled version of the Northrop Flying Wing

Some new planes can fly at 3,600 miles (5,760 kilometers) an hour—about six times the speed of sound!

In what ways are planes used today?

Small planes are used to check telephone lines and pipelines. They're used by photographers who want to take pictures from the sky. Flight instructors use light planes for flying lessons.

Airplanes are used by the armed forces. Some planes are big enough to carry tanks and large numbers of soldiers. Most military planes are bombers or fighter planes that are designed for sky battles.

Farmers use specially built planes to spray their crops against insect pests. These planes have large tanks to store chemicals. A Canadian plane that can suck up water from lakes is used to fight fires.

Some planes are designed for stunt flying and air races. And last, but not least, large airliners carry people and cargo all over the world.

United States Air Force Thunderbirds in formation flight

Who invented the helicopter?

About 500 years ago, a famous artist named Leonardo da Vinci (duh VIN-chee) designed the first helicopter. He drew pictures of it, but never built it. In 1939, Igor Sikorsky (EE-gore sih-CORE-skee) designed the first helicopter that worked. But an autogyro (AW-toe-JIE-row), an airplane with blades on top, was built by Juan de la Cierva (day lah see-AIR-vuh) in 1920. The blades were spun, not by the engine, but by the motion of the air as the plane traveled through it. Unlike our modern helicopter, the autogyro couldn't stay still in the air.

Sikorsky flying an early helicopter.

Why don't helicopters need big airports?

Helicopters can move straight up and down in the air. So they don't need a lot of space to take off and land. The place where they do take off and land is called a heliport. It may be on the ground, the roof of a building, or the deck of a ship.

How can a helicopter go straight up?

Instead of regular wings, a helicopter has three or more wing-like blades mounted on top of it. They are called rotor (ROE-tur) blades. They whirl around in a fast circle. The pressure of the air under the blades becomes greater than the pressure of the air on top. The greater pressure pushes upward on the blades, and the helicopter is lifted into the air. By changing the tilt, or angle, of the blades, the pilot can move the helicopter forward or backward. When the blades are not tilted, the helicopter can stay in one spot.

Is there any plane with wings that can fly straight up?

Yes, the convertiplane can fly straight up and down. It can take off and land like a helicopter. But once it is in the air, it flies like an airplane. Some convertiplanes have rotating blades on top. Those that don't, sometimes work by turning or tilting their wings or engines. Others use a special system of flaps and vanes. Convertiplanes cost more to build than regular airplanes.

Experimental McDonnell XV-1 Convertiplane

What is an amphibian?

An amphibian (am-FIB-ee-un) is an airplane that can land on ground or on water. The pilot pulls the wheels up in order to land the plane on water. The pilot lowers the wheels for a ground landing. This airplane was named after the animals known as amphibians. Animal amphibians live part of their lives in water and part on land. Frogs, toads, and salamanders are all amphibians.

278

What is a seaplane?

A seaplane is an airplane that can land and take off on water. It has floats instead of landing wheels.

How do some airplanes write in the sky?

When a metal called titanium (tie-TAY-nee-um) is mixed with chlorine gas, it makes smoke. A skywriting airplane carries this mixture in a tank. The pilot uses the plane like a "pen." He releases the smoke and flies in the pattern of the words he is spelling. The result is big, white letters in the sky.

279

How many scheduled airlines are there in the United States?

There are 35 scheduled airlines. They fly between 690 places around the world. A scheduled airline flies planes every day at fixed times. Non-scheduled airlines make up to ten round-trip flights a month. But they have no fixed time schedules. Feeder airlines are smaller airline companies that make only short flights. They fly between small towns or between small towns and large city airports.

View from a jet approaching a New York airport.

Scheduled airlines in the United States carry more than 200 million passengers a year!

POOR WOODSTOCK... WITH ALL THAT AIR TRAFFIC, HE'S AFRAID THEY MAY BAN THE BIRDS!!

How many airports are there in the United States?

There are about 13,000 airports in the United States. Of these, more than 4,000 are open to the general public. About 8,000 are privately owned and may be used only by members of a club. And more than 400 are military airports, open only to people in the armed forces.

What is the largest airport in the world?

The world's largest airport is the Dallas/Fort Worth Airport in Texas. It extends over an area of 17,500 acres (7,000 hectares). It is about the size of an average small city. When this airport is completed, it will have 9 runways, 13 terminals, and 260 gates. Sixty million passengers will come through the airport every year.

THE LONESOME COWBOY IS FAST BECOMING AN ENDANGERED SPECIES!

! When it opened in 1974, the Dallas/Fort Worth Airport had already cost seven hundred million dollars ($700,000,000)! **!**

What is the busiest airport in the world?

The world's busiest airport is the Chicago International Airport at O'Hare Field. In 1977, about 44 million passengers went through the Chicago International Airport. There were 749,278 takeoffs and landings. Day and night around the clock there was a takeoff or a landing about every 42 seconds.

How long does it take to build an airport?

It takes from 7 to 10 years before an airport is built and ready to handle passengers. Before an airport is built a master plan is prepared. The master plan shows how an airport will look 20 to 30 years in the future.

The airport is built a section at a time, according to the master plan. As soon as a section is completed it is opened to the public.

Why does an airplane need a runway?

An airplane needs a runway to take off and to land. An airplane must race across the ground to gather speed before the lift force is strong enough to raise it off the ground.

Small planes can leave the ground at speeds of only 30–40 miles (48–64 kilometers) an hour. That is slower than cars normally travel on a highway. Heavier planes may have to reach 100 miles (160 kilometers) an hour before they can lift into the air. That is almost twice the speed limit for cars on a highway.

Big airliners need a long runway to gain enough speed to take off. Some runways are more than a mile long. An airplane also needs a long runway to land and slow down to a stop.

What happens to a plane before it is ready to take off?

An airplane is thoroughly checked by the airline's safety crew before it is allowed to leave the airport. A person from the Federal Aviation Administration spot-checks the plane to be sure it is safe. Everything in the airplane must be working correctly. Mechanics who work on it are well trained. They know how to take an engine completely apart. They can put it together again so that it runs perfectly.

A "safety man" checks the weight of the baggage, the passengers, and the cargo. The dispatcher decides the route the pilot will take and how high up he should fly. The weather station tells the pilot what the weather conditions will be like during the flight.

The pilot and the flight crew check the instruments on the control panel. They use a check list. The pilot names an instrument. The co-pilot or flight engineer tests the instrument to be sure it is working right. The pilot starts the engines. He speaks to the control tower by radio. The control tower tells the pilot which runway to use.

What aircraft can go higher than jet planes?

Rockets can go higher than jet planes. Both rockets and jets need oxygen or their fuel won't burn. Jets must get their oxygen from the air. Since there is no air in outer space, they cannot fly there. Rockets contain their own oxygen so they can fly in outer space.

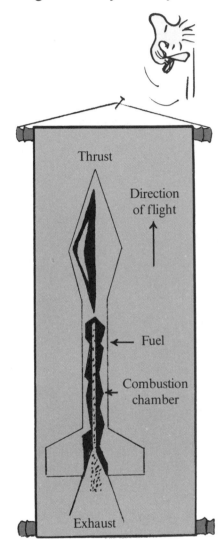

How does a rocket engine work?

A simple rocket engine is a tube closed at one end and open at the other end. It contains fuel and oxygen. The oxygen is needed to burn the fuel. When the fuel burns, it turns into a gas. The hot gas pushes out in all directions inside the rocket tube. It rushes out the open end. Gas rushing out in one direction pushes the rocket in the other direction. In rocket language, this push is called "thrust." The greater the thrust, the faster the rocket picks up speed.

You can see for yourself how a rocket works. Put a garden hose on flat ground. Turn on the water full force. The nozzle of the hose will be pushed backward as the water rushes out.

A rocket engine works much like a jet engine. But the jet engine must take in oxygen from the outside air to burn its fuel. The rocket carries its own oxygen supply.

What was the first rocket sent into space?

A Chinese youth in about the year 1200 put some chemicals in a tube and attached a fuse to it. He lit the fuse and fired the first skyrocket. It was like the rockets we use in Fourth of July fireworks. It could not travel very far.

Robert Goddard, an American scientist, sent up a new kind of rocket in 1926. It traveled as high as a 20-story building. But it wasn't until 1957 that a rocket reached what is called "outer space." That begins about 100 miles (160 kilometers) above the earth. This time the Russians were the successful ones. They sent Sputnik I into orbit around the world.

How fast can a modern rocket go?

Modern rockets are fast travelers. They usually race through space at 18,000–25,000 miles (29,000–40,000 kilometers) an hour. At the fastest of these speeds, you could circle the entire earth in only one hour!

Dr. Robert H. Goddard with an early rocket.

Apollo 15 Saturn V lifting off to the Moon on July 26, 1971.

Did Charlie Brown and Snoopy ever fly into outer space?

Yes! "Charlie Brown" and "Snoopy" were nicknames for parts of the Apollo 10 spacecraft. The Saturn V rocket lifted Apollo 10 into space.

Astronauts Young, Cernan, and Stafford sat in a part of the spacecraft called Charlie Brown. When they were 69 miles (110 kilometers) above the moon, Cernan and Stafford crawled through a tunnel to another part of the spacecraft. Now they were inside Snoopy.

Snoopy separated from Charlie Brown. Inside Snoopy, Cernan and Stafford came within 9 miles (more than 14 kilometers) of the moon. From there they took some pictures. Then Snoopy rejoined Charlie Brown, which was still flying around the moon. Cernan and Stafford climbed back into Charlie Brown.

Apollo 10 increased its speed. Snoopy was sent to fly around the moon alone. Charlie Brown and the astronauts headed towards Earth for a safe splashdown.

Apollo 10

⁑ SIGH ⁑

YOU'RE DEPRESSED BECAUSE THE SPACECRAFT NAMED AFTER YOU IS FLOATING ALONE IN SPACE!?!

How might people travel 100 years from now?

How does a flying umbrella sound to you? Or maybe you'd prefer a flying belt or a flying car to take you where you want to go. All of these may be possible 100 years from now.

By then a "flying saucer" could become a reality. It might be kept in the sky by streams of air that rush from the saucer-shaped vehicle. It would probably be able to travel through space, too.

Rocket ships powered by nuclear energy will probably be used a lot 100 years from now. These rocket ships would move very fast. They might even be able to reach other planets in only a few days' time.

Space stations in the sky may become as common as train stations are today. And space shuttles might carry you from one space stop to another.

Are flying saucers real?

Many reliable people have reported seeing strange sights in the sky. Some of these people said the objects looked like large saucers. Scientists call flying saucers **U**nidentified **F**lying **O**bjects, or UFOs. Most UFOs have turned out to be either the reflections of lights or natural space objects.

Sometimes clouds are shaped like huge saucers.

Meteors are often thought to be UFOs. Meteors are bright trails made by chunks of metal or stone that enter the earth's atmosphere from outer space. A meteor usually burns up completely as it moves through the air. Any piece that reaches the ground is called a meteorite.

Some UFOs were really fireballs—very bright meteors. Some fireballs explode. Pieces of the fireball may fall to earth. A fireball can look as bright as a star or even as bright as the moon.

Comets have been mistaken for UFOs, too. A comet is a huge mass of frozen gas, ice, and dust. The comet travels around the sun in a definite path. We can see a comet only when it comes near the earth. A comet looks like a fuzzy star with a long tail. Sometimes the tail is millions of miles long.

Some UFOs don't seem to have any explanation. But so far, no one has proven that any of these UFOs were spaceships from other planets.

288

Did You Know That...

The first successful balloon flight across the Atlantic Ocean began in a clover field in Presque Isle, Maine. It was there that Ben Abruzzo, Maxie Anderson, and Larry Newman filled their *Double Eagle II* with helium on August 11, 1978. They drifted eastward in an open gondola. It was quite cold and sometimes they were as high as four miles above the ocean. Six days later they landed in a wheat field in Miserey, France. The three had traveled nonstop for more than 3,000 miles by balloon—a world's record!

Double Eagle II

At a busy airport, more than 2,000 airplanes may take off or land in one day. With so much air traffic, airports need controllers to act as "traffic police." Controllers keep track of every aircraft from a tall control tower. They can contact pilots by two-way radio. A pilot must have permission from a controller to take off, land, or even taxi up to the terminal. Controllers follow planes in the air on radar screens. Any plane within 50 miles of the control tower will show up on the screen.

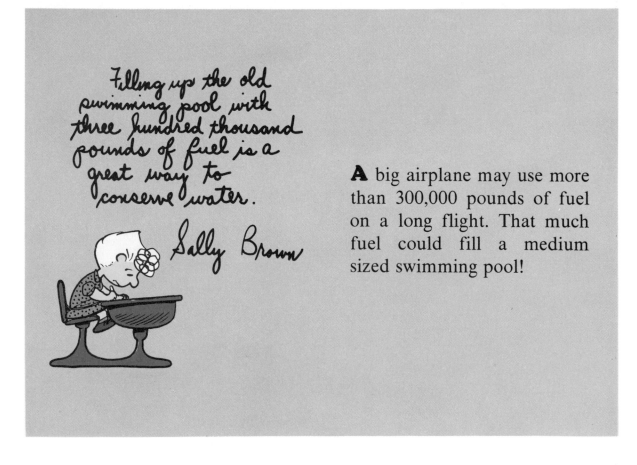

A big airplane may use more than 300,000 pounds of fuel on a long flight. That much fuel could fill a medium sized swimming pool!

Many people have managed to swim across the English Channel. But Bryan Allen was the first to pedal his way across in an airplane. His plane, the *Gossamer Albatross*, was made of plastic and piano wire. For nearly three hours in June 1979 he pumped the pedals that turned the propeller. The 23 mile channel trip was the longest human-powered flight in history.

Gossamer Albatross